TALES OF THE DEAD

ANCIENT GREECE

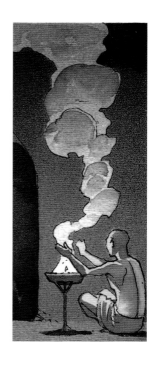
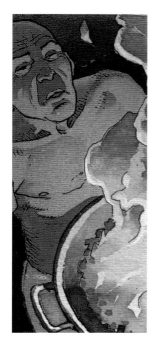

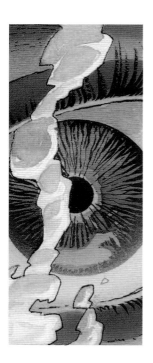

Written by Stewart Ross
Consultant Hugh Bowden
Illustrated by Inklink & Richard Bonson

LONDON, NEW YORK, MUNICH,
MELBOURNE AND DELHI

SENIOR EDITOR Simon Beecroft
ART EDITOR/STORY VISUALISER John Kelly
ART DIRECTOR Mark Richards
PUBLISHING MANAGER Cynthia O'Neill Collins
PUBLISHER Alex Kirkham
PRODUCTION CONTROLLER Erica Rosen
DTP DESIGNER Dean Scholey

First published in Great Britain in 2004 by
Dorling Kindersley Limited, 80 Strand, London WC2R 0RL
A Penguin Company

04 05 06 07 08 10 9 8 7 6 5 4 3 2

A CIP record for this book is available from the British Library.

ISBN 1-4053-0368-9

Colour reproduction by Colourscan, Singapore
Printed and bound by Leo Paper Products, China

Discover more at
www.dk.com

ACKNOWLEDGMENTS

Richard Bonson painted the agora (pages 10–11), Delphic oracle (pages 14–15), theatre (pages 18–19),
Athens' harbour (pages 22–23), and Olympic games (pages 28–29).

Inklink painted all other artworks, including the graphic novel.

Dorling Kindersley would like to thank Rob Reichenfeld for the Parthenon photograph (page 4).

CONTENTS

DEADLY RIVALRY

Ancient Greece was one of the richest civilisations the world had ever seen. Its culture spread as far west as North Africa and Spain, and as far east as India. Even today, a great deal of Western language, politics, art and thinking can all be traced back to the remarkable Greeks.

Some 2,400 years ago, Greece was torn by war. Athens was the most powerful city in all of Greece. For 10 years, the other cities, led by Sparta, attempted to bring down Athens. Even when the fighting stopped, Athens and Sparta went on competing. It was not just in war that they looked for victory…

MIGHTY TEMPLE

One of the most famous buildings in the world is the temple of the Parthenon. For more than 2,000 years, it has stood on a hill high above the city of Athens in Greece. In ancient times, the people of Athens made their way up the hill to the temple to worship the goddess Athene.

MEET THE CHARACTERS…

PYLADES
"At school I get teased for talking about my big brother Kinesias all the time. Fair enough, but I really am proud of him. He's the clear favourite to win the Olympic race-in-armour – just brilliant!"

KALONIKE
"I know I'm only a thirteen-year-old girl who spends her life indoors and doesn't know about sports – but I have been educated. My mother saw to that. So maybe I'll be able to help my brother Kinesias some day?"

KINESIAS
"I don't reckon anyone could have trained harder for success in the Olympic Games than I have done over the last year. I'm under a lot of pressure, though – all Athens is depending on me. Not to mention my eleven-year-old brother!"

TIMELINE

1969
American astronauts land on the Moon

1492
Columbus sails to America

1275
Genghis Khan conquers Asia

570 CE
Birth of Muhammad, founder of Islam

146 BCE
Romans seize control of mainland Greece

507
World's first democracy emerges in Athens

4

PRESENT DAY

2000 CE (COMMON ERA)   1000 CE   CE   BCE

THE PRICE OF VICTORY

Our story takes place in 416 BCE. Athens and Sparta are at peace with each other, and the Olympic Games are shortly to be held. As you read on, pick up on the details of life in ancient Greece, from clothing and diet to buildings and the belief in unreliable, short-tempered gods and goddesses.

SPARTA.

EARLY EVENING.

A SECRET MEETING IS ABOUT TO TAKE PLACE...

WE ARE HERE TO DISCUSS THE FORTHCOMING GAMES...

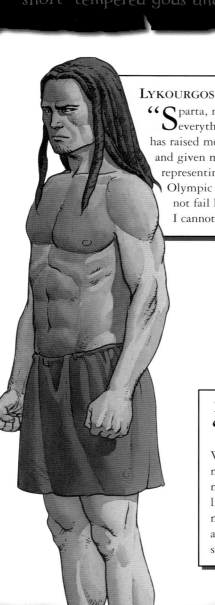

LYKOURGOS

"**S**parta, my native city, is everything to me. She has raised me, trained me and given me the honour of representing her at the Olympic Games. I must not fail her… I cannot fail her!"

MYRTILOS

"**I** don't want Olympic glory. What I want is money, enough to lift me out of my wretched life as a theatre odd-job man. I dream of owning a little farm somewhere…."

THE GREEK WORLD

Ancient Greece was a pleasant land. Rocky mountains rose above broad plains dotted with low, sunbaked farms and shady groves of olive trees. Cities surrounded by high walls perched on high hills. The coast had a thousand natural harbours. From them Greece was linked to the known world via the blue highway of the Mediterranean Sea.

NORTH AMERICA
EUROPE
ASIA
SOUTH AMERICA
AFRICA

MACEDONIA

• Mount Olympos

• Troy

ASIA MINOR (modern-day Turkey)

Delphi •

Olympia •

• Athens

GREECE

Sparta •

KOS

Mediterranean Sea

CRETE

AFRICA

776
First Olympic Games are held (according to tradition)

*c.*1400
Civilisation emerges on mainland Greece around the city of Mycenae

*c.*2000
Earliest Greek-style civilisation develops on the island of Crete

*c.*2500
Indus Valley civilization flourishes in Pakistan

*c.*3100
King Menes unites Egypt

1000 BCE (BEFORE COMMON ERA)   2000 BCE   3000 BCE

CONTINUED FROM PREVIOUS PAGE ➤

...WE **MUST** WIN THE RACE-IN-ARMOUR...

FOR THE HONOUR OF **SPARTA**.

IT IS THE RACE WITH THE **GREATEST GLORY** FOR A WARRIOR PEOPLE.

YOU HEAR, LYKOURGOS?

ATHENS

Athene was the patron goddess of Athens.

In ancient times, Greece was made up of many independent cities that ruled the surrounding areas. The wealthiest and most powerful of these city-states was Athens, with its surrounding territory of Attica. Athens was a great centre of the arts and learning. The Athenians lived on the land below a rocky hill, or Acropolis, that was crowned with a grand temple called the Parthenon.

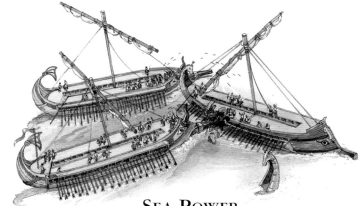

SEA POWER
With its large navy, Athens ruled the sea and became wealthy through trade and fighting in foreign lands. Its fleet consisted of over 300 triple-decked, oar-powered ramming ships, called *triremes*.

The Parthenon

Men and women wore cloth tunics called *chitons*.

Slaves were not allowed to cut their hair.

SERVING THE MASTERS
Slaves did all the hard work for the free citizens (you could only be a citizen if you had parents who were citizens).

GROWING UP
Boys went to school to learn to become citizens while girls stayed at home to learn domestic skills.

WOMEN'S WORK
Women's lives were severely restricted in Athens. Citizen women ran their husband's household.

DOING YOUR DUTY
All male Athenian citizens – from philosophers to merchants – had to be ready to fight for the state at any time.

I WILL **WIN**, SIR – FOR SPARTA!

THE SHAME OF LOSING WOULD BE UNBEARABLE.

MYRTILOS?

MYRTILOS AT YOUR SERVICE, SIR...

STAGEHAND, SPY...

...REMOVER OF **NUISANCES**!

JUST WHAT'S NEEDED. WILL YOU HELP ME, MYRTILOS?

MAYBE, LYKOURGOS...

SPARTA

The Spartans honoured Artemis, goddess of hunting.

Of all the Greek city-states, only Sparta could match the power of Athens. Sparta was organised like an army. It waged wars of defence and conquest, and ruled over the non-Spartans within its territory. Spartans did not appreciate Athens' fine buildings, drama and philosophy. What they really valued was the rigour, toughness, and bravery of a true warrior.

TRAINED ARMY
Male Spartans were full-time, professional soldiers of the state. Highly trained Spartan footsoldiers, called hoplites, lived and fought together and were the most feared troops in the land – and beyond.

Spartan soldiers wore crimson cloaks on the battlefield to hide blood stains.

SPARTAN SOLDIERS
In Sparta, the authorities provided men with land to live on, as well as a wife to farm the land and raise children.

SPARTAN WOMEN
Spartan women were the freest in all Greece. They were encouraged to do sports and athletics.

RAISED TO FIGHT
At the age of seven, Spartan boys were forced to live in army barracks and learn the arts of war.

SLAVES AND SERVANTS
The Spartans ruled over the local people, called *helots* and *perioikoi*, whose land they had conquered.

BUT HE NEEDN'T FEAR **MUCH LONGER**.

HMM, I CAN SEE WHY LYKOURGOS IS WORRIED.

THE SPARTANS SHOULD **WATCH OUT**!

HE WILL BE THE **GLORY** OF **ATHENS**.

AH, **THAT'S BETTER**! NOW, WHAT DO YOU WANT?

KINESIAS THE ATHENIAN MUST NOT COMPETE IN THE GAMES...

BY ANY MEANS – **STOP HIM**!

I WILL HEAD FOR **ATHENS** AT FIRST LIGHT!

FOR **SPARTA**!

IN ATHENS...

GO KINESIAS, FOR **ATHENS**!

EVERY DAY AFTER SCHOOL I WATCH MY BROTHER KINESIAS....

FOR ATHENS, PYLADES!

...TRAINING FOR THE GAMES.

7

CONTINUED FROM PREVIOUS PAGE

MIND AND BODY

The Ancient Greeks appreciated the good life, and often held lavish parties. But they also kept fit, and explored science, maths and philosophy far further than previous civilisations. Much of life today – from the Olympic Games to science and medicine – rests on Ancient Greek foundations.

A slave beats olives from the branches before gathering them in baskets.

HEALTH FOOD

Olive oil, used in cooking, was essential to the Greeks' healthy lifestyles.

Olive oil was also burned in lamps.

Slaves crush ripe olives in huge presses to release the precious oil.

THE SYMPOSIUM

The favourite Greek party was the symposium. These evenings of drinking and talking were held in private houses after a meal. A person known as a *symposiarch* guided the discussion and controlled the flow of wine. Entertainment was provided by musicians and dancers. Most symposiums were quite serious, with guests talking about important political and philosophical topics. But some got out of hand with rowdy games, drinking songs – and worse!

Wine was made from grapes

A slave brings tasty tit-bits, such as roasted grasshopper.

Wine jug, called an *oinochoe*

Guests lay two to a couch.

I WENT TO GREET KINESIAS AFTER TRAINING.

YOU LOOKED **INVINCIBLE**, BROTHER.

ONLY THE **GODS** ARE INVINCIBLE, PYLADES.

UNCLE'S SYMPOSIUM TONIGHT, REMEMBER?

OF COURSE! I'M YOUR CHAPERONE.

WE WALKED TO UNCLE'S HOUSE.

IT WAS ONLY MY **SECOND** SYMPOSIUM...

...AND I WAS REALLY LOOKING FORWARD TO IT.

WELCOME, SIRS.

UNCLE'S OTHER GUESTS WERE ALREADY EATING AND TALKING.

JAVELIN THROWING

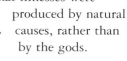
ALL-IN WRESTLING

SPRINTING

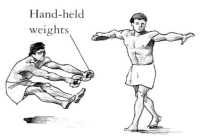
Hand-held weights

LONG-JUMP   DISCUS THROWING

GETTING BETTER

One of Greece's most important discoveries was scientific medicine. In the late fifth century BCE, a doctor called Hippokrates founded a medical school on the island of Kos. He was the first to argue that illnesses were produced by natural causes, rather than by the gods.

Medical instruments

Wine was usually drunk mixed with water.

A slave girl plays the pipes to entertain the guests.

GREAT GAMES

The highlights of the Greek sporting calendar were the athletic games held in various states, but most famously every four years in Olympia – the Olympic Games. Professional athletes competed in honour of the gods – and to out-do their rivals from other states. There were horse and chariot races, and many events similar to those of a modern track and field meeting.

LEARNING THE RHYTHM

Only young male citizens went to school. For seven days a week they studied a core curriculum of literacy, music and physical education. Music was more than just a subject – it reflected the rhythms of life itself and was a key part of all festivals and ceremonies. Not surprisingly, the warlike Spartans had little time for literacy or music. They concentrated instead on physical training, fighting and hunting.

STORY CONTINUES ON NEXT PAGE

SIGNED BY ATHENE!

"I HAVE SPOKEN..."

"ATTEND NOT THE GAMES, KINESIAS."

WHAT'S THIS?

KINESIAS WAS THE CENTRE OF ATTENTION.

WHEN YOU **WIN** THE **RACE-IN-ARMOUR**, KINESIAS...

EXCUSE ME, SIR...

...BUT **ATHENE** ALONE CAN GRANT ME VICTORY.

WE LEFT IN GOOD TIME.

GOOD NIGHT!

JUST OUTSIDE THE DOOR, ONE OF UNCLE'S SLAVES GAVE KINESIAS A SLATE.

A STRANGER HANDED IT TO ME, SIR...

THE AGORA

Near the middle of every Greek city lay a bustling market square known as the agora. The agora in Athens was the busiest and most exciting of all. In the mornings, it was crammed with shopkeepers' stalls – you can just imagine the din! Sometimes the stalls were cleared away to make room for a special religious or political occasion. The government of Athens was also carried out in temples, law courts and other buildings in the agora.

NEXT MORNING, I WAS STILL TROUBLED ABOUT THE MESSAGE.

WHAT'S THAT?

NOTHING, SISTER.

NEVER MIND, I'LL GO AND ASK MOTHER...

NO! CAN YOU KEEP A SECRET?

OF COURSE!

THEN READ!

1 EARLY START
The rows of stalls were laid out like a modern supermarket – cheese down one aisle, meat down another, and so on. There were even aisles for books and second-hand clothes. The stall keeper paid a fee to reserve his place and arrived at dawn to get everything set up before the eager shoppers arrived.

2 MONEY MATTERS
Bankers lent money and exchanged the coins from other cities to the ones used in Athens. The rate of exchange was supposed to depend on the weight of precious metal in the coins. However, crooked bankers always found a way of swindling their customers – often by using scales that didn't weigh correctly.

3 NO CHEATING
City officers patrolled the market to make sure the goods that people sold were of the right quality and sold in the correct quantities. They also made sure that rubbish did not block the roads.

4 MAIN STREET
The city's main street was called the Panathenaic Way. It ran through the middle of the agora, from a gate in the city walls all the way to the Acropolis.

10 MAKING MONEY
Athens' famous coins were made in this heavily-guarded building. Trusted workmen melted down bars of silver and poured the liquid metal into moulds. One side was stamped with the head of Athene, the other side carried her symbol, an owl.

KALONIKE WAS AS FRIGHTENED AS WE WERE.

IF THIS IS TRUE, THE GODDESS WILL SURELY GIVE YOU A SIGN.

ALL DAY LONG, I WAS LOOKING FOR A SIGN.

KALONIKE'S WORDS HAUNTED ME...

AN OWL IN DAYTIME?

THE OWL WAS A SIGN OF ATHENE!

THIS WAS A BAD OMEN.

STORY CONTINUES ON NEXT PAGE ▶

8 THE FOUNTAIN HOUSE

Athenian women would walk to the fountain house to gather water for their homes. Water was piped into the city from a distant mountain spring.

7 SOUTH STOA

A stoa was like a modern covered market, except that it could also be a museum and an art gallery. All kinds of citizens – from teachers to sweet-makers – sheltered here from the sun or rain. They did business deals or just stood about chatting.

9 LAW COURT

Law courts were large buildings where as many as 501 citizens decided whether a person accused of a crime was guilty or not. Before the decision, citizens made speeches that set out both sides of the case. The law courts were often open-air.

6 LUCKY TEMPLE

Craftsworkers looking for work would gather near the Temple of Hephaistos, the god of fire and metal working. These labourers wanted the god's help and protection. Many bronze and iron working foundries were also built around the temple.

5 FARM PRODUCE

A farmer has set out a makeshift stall of home-made goods. On display are live pigs, charcoal, cheese, wine and blankets woven by his wife from the wool they have cut from their sheep.

IT WAS A STATUE...

...OF ATHENE!

WHAT WAS IT?

...FROM THE WINDOW ABOVE.

I CHASED IT THROUGH THE AGORA.

PYLADES?

PYLADES! WHERE ARE YOU GOING?

KINESIAS!

THEN I SAW IT...

LOOK OUT!

11

CONTINUED FROM PREVIOUS PAGE

OUR SISTER WAS **RIGHT**.

THIS WAS THE SIGN KALONIKE WARNED OF.

A WARNING?

WE MUST FIND OUT.

GODS AND GODDESSES

The Greeks believed in many gods and goddesses. The most important and powerful was Zeus, the King of the Gods. He and 11 others were said to live on the top of Mount Olympos, the highest peak in Greece. The Greeks believed their deities (gods and goddesses) were like ordinary human beings – except more powerful and often more difficult to please.

ATHENE

Athene was the goddess of wisdom and household crafts. She was said to have appeared, fully grown, out of Zeus' head. Athene was fond of a certain city in Greece, so gave its citizens the gift of an olive tree, which produced food, oil and wood. Athene named this city Athens.

ARTEMIS

The moon goddess Artemis lived with the other gods and goddesses on the top of Mount Olympos. She was a mighty hunter and the guardian of all women. She was armed with a bow and arrows, and had a wickedly short temper.

ZEUS AND HERE

Zeus was the ruler of all the gods on Mount Olympos. He threw thunderbolts and lightning at anyone who broke his laws. Here was the goddess of married women. She was Zeus' wife, even though she was also his sister. Zeus tricked her into marriage – and she was unhappy with him ever after!

WE CONSULTED A SOOTHSAYER...

...ONE WHO IS SAID TO BE ABLE TO TELL THE **FUTURE**!

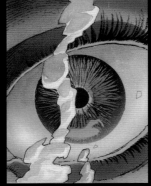

Winged cap

HERMES

Zeus' son Hermes was the super-energetic messenger of the gods. He had wings on his sandals, cap and staff, so he could fly. Hermes was known for being clever and quick-thinking.

HEPHAISTOS
The god of fire and metal-working, Hephaistos made weapons for the other gods.

DEMETER
The farmers' favourite, Demeter was responsible for the growth of crops, plants and fruit.

APOLLO
Another of Zeus' sons, Apollo was the god of music, as well as fortune-telling, truth and the Sun.

DIONYSOS
Dionysos was the god of wine, parties and new life. He was also the god of Greek theatre.

ARES
Ares was the awesome god of war. He didn't care which side won, so long as blood was shed.

APHRODITE
Flowers grew wherever Aphrodite walked. She was the goddess of love and beauty.

PAN

The god Pan was believed to dwell deep in the woodlands of central Greece. He spent his time playing pipes, looking after shepherds and chasing pretty girls. But he was not just a pipe-playing lover – when he got angry he could fill men with wild terror. This gives us our word 'panic'.

Poseidon's magical trident

POSEIDON

Anyone wanting to sail across the seas first prayed to the mighty Poseidon. He was the god of sea and earthquakes. Poseidon lived beneath the waves in a huge palace made of coral and gems. He could create shipwrecks by striking the ground with a three-pronged staff called a trident.

HADES

In Greek mythology, when the world was divided, Zeus got the heavens and Poseidon got the sea. Zeus' grim brother Hades was given the Underworld, where the souls of the dead lived in misery. Hades sat on a throne made of ivory while his three-headed guard dog Kerberos allowed new spirits in, but let none leave.

STORY CONTINUES ON NEXT PAGE →

THERE'S ALWAYS THE **ORACLE** AT DELPHI.

THE MIGHTY **APOLLO** WILL NOT FAIL US.

USELESS! ALL OF THEM, **USELESS!**

...THE GODS ARE UNCLEAR...

...WHO CAN TELL?

I CANNOT BE SURE...

HE WASN'T MUCH USE.

WE **HAVE** TO KNOW!

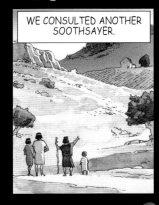

WE CONSULTED ANOTHER SOOTHSAYER.

PERHAPS IT IS A WARNING...

...OR PERHAPS NOT.

13

CONTINUED FROM PREVIOUS PAGE

WE LEFT AT ONCE FOR THE **TEMPLE OF APOLLO** AT **DELPHI**.

BRRR! I'M FREEZING

IT'S NOT HELPING MY **FITNESS** MUCH, EITHER

HA! MY PLAN IS WORKING. HE'LL BE IN NO FIT STATE TO COMPETE.

1 APOLLO'S TEMPLE

The Temple of Apollo housed the famous oracle. Apollo was the god of light and music, and one of the most popular oracle gods. He was said to have first arrived at Delphi in the form of a dolphin – which is how the town got its name.

2 INFALLIBLE ORACLE

The Pythia was a middle-aged woman who dressed in young girl's clothes. When she contacted Apollo, she went into a trance, which may have been caused by fasting or by gases seeping into the chamber.

3 ATHENIAN TREASURY

The city of Athens built this marble vault to store treasures in. The valuables were brought out on special occasions such as sacred processions or athletic games.

4 SACRED WAY

The road that zigzagged up to the oracle was lined with monuments and statues, built by visitors in honour of Apollo. The Greek city-states competed to raise the most impressive buildings.

5 THE SIBYL'S ROCK

Stories were told about the Delphic Sibyl. She was said to have sat on a rock in a trance and sang her predictions for the future. Many people believed that she was the daughter of sea monsters.

8 THEATRE AND SPORTS

Drama and musical contests were also held at Delphi in a theatre on the mountainside. At the same time, outside the holy oracle areas, athletic contests like those at Olympia took place.

DELPHI.

THE CENTRE OF THE WORLD.

WE OBEYED THE **RITUALS**

AND **SACRIFICED** A GOAT.

THE SIGNS WERE **FAVOURABLE** SO WE WERE ADMITTED TO THE TEMPLE.

WE WERE LED TO THE **CHAMBER OF THE ORACLE**...

7 SAFETY FIRST
The buildings around the oracle were packed with riches. This made them tempting targets for thieves. To keep marauders out, the entire area was surrounded by a high wall.

6 GOOD OMEN
When people arrived to consult the oracle, the priests would present a goat to Apollo. If the animal trembled, this meant the god was ready to speak. In the ceremony the goat was sprinkled with water beforehand so it was very likely to shiver.

THE DELPHIC ORACLE

The town of Delphi, nestling on the slopes of mighty Mount Parnassos, was home to the most famous oracle in Ancient Greece. Oracles were 'hotlines' to the gods – the Greeks visited them when they had important questions they wanted answering. People queued up to give their question to a priestess, called a Pythia, who went into a trance to find out the god's will. Her answers could determine when farmers planted their fields or when an empire declared war.

BUT TO HONOUR ATHENE YOU MUST **STAY AT HOME!**

I'M TRAPPED!

TO HONOUR ZEUS I MUST **GO TO THE GAMES.**

IT WAS OVER.

AND WITH THAT...

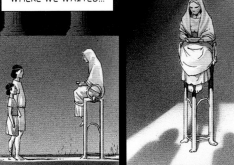

WHERE WE WAITED...

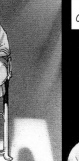

WHILE THE **PRIESTESS** COMMUNED WITH THE GODS.

FINALLY, SHE SPOKE.

HEAR YE, THE WORDS OF **APOLLO**...

YOU MUST **ALWAYS** HONOUR THE GODS.

CONTINUED FROM PREVIOUS PAGE ➤

PLAYS AND ACTING

Greek plays were religious events as well as entertainment. They grew out of song and dance routines that were a part of worship, particularly of the wine god Dionysos. In Kinesias' time, each play featured just three main actors, who played all the parts. A larger group of actors, called the chorus, spoke to the audience about the action.

Masks were made of a kind of pottery called terracotta.

Male actors dressed as women to play female roles.

Actors wore big wigs and platform shoes to make themselves look larger on stage.

MASKED MASTERS

Only men appeared on the Greek stage. Even women's parts were played by male actors. There was no chance of becoming a pin-up celebrity, however – all actors performed in masks. This was so that one actor could play several parts. The exaggerated expressions on the masks also made it easier for those seated at the back to see.

SERIOUS PLAYS

The first true plays were 'tragedies'. They were serious stories about characters who were punished for doing wrong – or just for making a mistake. In the play *Oedipus the King*, Oedipus does both: without knowing who they are, he kills his father and marries his mother!

CHORUS LINE

As well as the three actors on the stage, Greek plays had a chorus of 15 men who stood at the front of the stage. In tragedies, the chorus commented on the events of the play. Sometimes they explained what was going on to the audience. The chorus in a comedy was much more fun. They sometimes pretended to be birds, wasps or even clouds.

The chorus sang, danced or spoke from a stage in front of the main actors.

WE RETURNED HOME...

TIRED...

AND ALL OUT OF IDEAS

BUT **KALONIKE** WASN'T GIVING UP THAT EASILY.

COME ON!

DON'T SIT THERE FEELING **SORRY** FOR YOURSELVES.

GO BACK TO THE PLACE THE STATUE FELL.

SEE WHAT YOU CAN **FIND** OUT.

I **HATE** IT WHEN SHE'S RIGHT.

OF COURSE I'M **RIGHT**.

THIS IS THE PLACE.

LET'S ASK.

SATYR PLAYS

Satyr plays were humorous performances based on stories from Greek myths. They featured assorted gods and heroes. The chorus always dressed as satyrs – legendary half-goat and half-human creatures who were the servants of Dionysos, the god of wine. Satyr plays were performed after a whole day of tragedies, to give the audience some light relief.

HO-HO!

Comedies poked fun at everyday life. The actors and chorus dressed up in ridiculous, exaggerated costumes. The main characters often stood for well-known types of people, such as drunken old men or angry women. The liveliest comedies were written by Aristophanes (448-385 BCE). He mocked everyone: men, women, politicians, thinkers – even the gods and goddesses.

The chorus in a comedy made the audience laugh with their horse-play!

Padded trousers helped create a humorous look

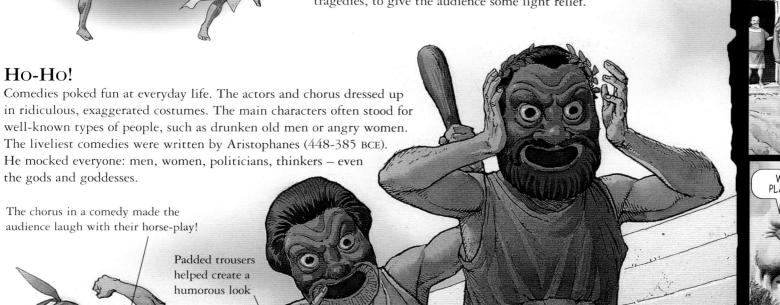

STORY CONTINUES ON NEXT PAGE

CONTINUED FROM PREVIOUS PAGE

THE THEATRE

The Greeks were the first people to put on plays in specially built theatres. All their theatres were in the open air, with as many as 80 rows of seats cut into the hillside and arranged in a semi-circle. They were so well designed that even the people at the back could hear the actors on stage, almost 80 metres (260 feet) away.

1 SACRIFICE

Because plays were religious events, animals were often sacrificed before the play began. The main theatre competition in Athens, for example, began with the sacrifice of oxen on an altar.

2 BRINGING DOWN THE GODS

Although actors couldn't move about much on the small stage, some of them could fly! The largest theatres used a crane, or *mechane*, to lower actors dressed as gods onto the stage, or swing heroes into action.

3 SANCTUARY OF DIONYSOS

The theatre was in an area sacred to Dionysos, the god of wine and new life. He was also the god of things not being what they appeared to be (illusions) – precisely what acting and theatres were all about.

WE ARRIVED AT THE **THEATRE**.

THE **AUDIENCE** WERE TAKING THEIR SEATS.

LET'S FIND THE **STAGE MANAGER**.

HE'S OVER THERE.

...I'M VERY BUSY NOW...

COME BACK LATER...

HEY!

WAIT!

STOP!

OUT OF OUR WAY!

YOU YOUNG ROGUE!

STOP HIM!

STORY CONTINUES ON NEXT PAGE

8 HARD BENCHES

Theatre seats were originally made of wood. In the best theatres, however, the audience sat on stone benches. The main theatre in Athens could seat about 17,000 spectators.

7 V.I.P. SEATS

The seats in the front row were reserved for special guests. These included city officials and priests. In Athens, the seat in the centre was reserved for the priest of Dionysos.

6 DANCING PLACE

The chorus danced and sang on a curved area before the stage known as the *orchestra*. This meant 'dancing place'. In English the word has come to mean something quite different: a large musical band.

5 SETTING THE SCENE

The actors performed on a small stage between the orchestra and the low building behind. The front of this building was known as the *skene* from which we get our words 'scene' and 'scenery'.

4 BEHIND THE SCENES

The building behind the acting area, originally just a tent, was where the actors changed into their costumes and masks and prepared for the performance.

HEY!

THUG!

HE WAS GETTING AWAY.

HE PUSHED SOMEONE ASIDE...

OOOF!

WHO REACHED OUT FOR SOMETHING TO HOLD ONTO.

PEOPLE POWER

Most Greek cities were ruled by the richest men in them. But in the sixth century BCE, the citizens of Athens tried something different. They shared power between everyone. The new system was called democracy, meaning 'people power'. It was not like a modern democracy because only male citizens were included. Even so, Athens' system of democracy lasted 200 years and influenced the way we govern ourselves today.

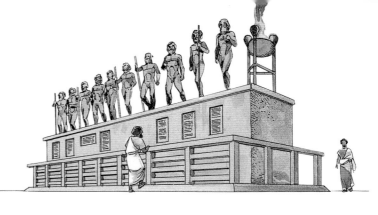

INFORMATION CENTRE

Athens was made up of 10 'tribes', based on the villages in which people lived. Each tribe was named after an ancient hero. The monument to these heroes was a popular meeting place in the city centre. It was also where government information, such as new laws, was displayed.

THE CITIZENS' ASSEMBLY

All male citizens could attend the full Assembly, known as the *ekklesia*, that met about 40 times a year. Those present voted, with a show of hands, whether to accept or reject ideas on how their city was run.

PROOF OF IDENTITY

Officials and citizens often carried their personal seal. A seal was a metal stamp that was pressed onto a lump of warm wax, lead or clay and stuck to a letter or document to prove it was genuine.

The Assembly was as likely to include fishermen as aristocrats.

THE COUNCIL

The Council, or *Boule*, proposed new policies and laws for the Assembly to discuss. It consisted of 500 men drawn equally from the 10 tribes that made up the Athenian citizen body.

THE THEATRE WAS IN **UPROAR**.

BUT KINESIAS AND I HAD SOMETHING.

HE DROPPED HIS **SEAL**.

I THINK IT'S SPARTAN.

DID YOU HEAR? I SAID **SPARTAN**...

OH...

HELLO FATHER...

...MAGISTRATE GOPOLOS...

...COUNCIL MEMBERS.

WHAT'S GOING ON HERE, MY SON?

THE ASSASSIN DROPPED **THIS**.

ASSASSIN?

STORY CONTINUES ON NEXT PAGE →

OUTVOTED

The Athenians were keen to make sure no one overturned their system of democracy. They had a procedure for getting rid of people who might be a threat. Each citizen wrote a name on a piece of pottery. These were then thrown into a special area. The man with the most votes was sent away from the city for 10 years – this was called being ostracised.

ATHENS HAS BECOME TOO DANGEROUS.

WE MUST GET HIM TO **OLYMPIA** AS SOON AS POSSIBLE.

COURT MASTERS

The law courts were run by nine men called *archons*. They were chosen from among the Athenian tribes. A man worked as an *archon* for a year, and only once in his lifetime. Some of the archons had special jobs. One dealt with unlawful killing, for instance, while another looked after matters concerning non citizens.

AND **MAKE SURE** HE WINS.

Open disc (guilty)

Solid disc (not guilty)

DISC JOCKEYS

Athenians also voted on whether someone was guilty of a crime or not. A group of at least 201 citizens (known as the jury) heard the case. After they had listened to what everyone had to say, each member of the jury was given two bronze discs. One was solid, which stood for not guilty; the other had a hole in the middle, which stood for guilty. The jury voted by dropping their discs into special pots.

NO! OUR PRIORITY IS TO PROTECT KINESIAS...

Juries voted by placing tokens into the pot marked for their tribe.

WE THOUGHT KINESIAS WAS BEING WARNED BY **ATHENE**.

BUT IT WAS A **SPARTAN SPY**.

THEY MEAN TO **STOP HIM COMPETING**.

THIS IS WORRYING NEWS INDEED.

GENTLEMEN, MY SON'S LIFE IS CLEARLY IN **DANGER**.

WE SHOULD TEACH THOSE SPARTANS A LESSON.

21

ATHENS' HARBOUR

The port of Peiraieus lay eight kilometres (five miles) southwest of Athens. The harbour was the city's lifeline, linking it to the outside world. It was so important that the road to Athens was defended by stone walls so that the city and its port were one huge fortress. Most of Athens' trade passed through Peiraieus harbour, and it was also the base of an enormous fleet of warships.

1 WARSHIPS
The fastest Greek ship, called a *trireme*, was rowed by up to 200 men. They sat in three levels, one above the other, on both sides of the ship.

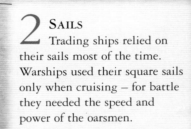

2 SAILS
Trading ships relied on their sails most of the time. Warships used their square sails only when cruising – for battle they needed the speed and power of the oarsmen.

3 SEA BATTLES
In battle, Greek triremes (warships) tried to sink enemy ships by using the sharp, bronze-tipped bow (front) to ram into the other vessels' sides.

4 SHIPS IN HARBOUR
Fishing ships and merchant ships came in all sorts of shapes and sizes. Merchant ships carried cargoes such as wine, oil, or grain in their deep holds.

5 MERCHANTS
As the largest port in all Greece, Peiraieus attracted merchants from every corner of the Mediterranean. Its streets and stalls echoed with the sound of bargaining in dozens of different languages. City officials collected a tax of two percent of the value of all goods passing through the port.

CONTINUED FROM PREVIOUS PAGE

LATER, AT A SECRET LOCATION...

MYRTILOS?

I BRING YOU NEWS...

SPEAK!

I FOLLOWED THEM...

TO THE DOCKS.

THEY LEAVE **TOMORROW** FOR OLYMPIA.

THEN WE MUST **WORK FAST.**

LATER.

I WANT THE MONEY NOW.

HALF NOW...

HALF WHEN THEY'VE **DROWNED.**

RIGHT HERE I THINK...

STORY CONTINUES ON NEXT PAGE

8 BOAT SHEDS
When not in action, the expensive triremes were hauled from the sea and stored in huge wooden sheds. Here they could be repaired and protected until needed again.

7 BUSY TOWN
Peiraieus was a huge commercial centre. The city had two agoras (market places) and two theatres. Ships from throughout the Mediterranean Sea docked here with their cargoes of merchandise for the Athenians.

6 TEMPLE
Sailors often entered a local temple at the end of a safe voyage to offer thanks to the gods.

FAR BEHIND...

LEAVING ALL OUR WORRIES...

FOR OLYMPIA.

BELOW THE WATERLINE.

THAT SHOULD FIX IT.

THE NEXT DAY.

KINESIAS, FATHER AND I SAID OUR GOODBYES...

GOOD LUCK, KINESIAS.

AND SET SAIL...

CONTINUED FROM PREVIOUS PAGE ▶

A BUSY PEOPLE

Most Greeks were farmers, although the dry, rocky land they worked on only produced enough to feed their own families. Yet city-states like Athens became immensely rich and powerful. Most of their wealth came from making things and trading with foreign lands. Greek traders went from place to place finding the best goods to bring back home.

ROUND TRIP

Merchant vessels were called 'round' or 'hollow' ships. Unlike the longer and narrower oar-driven warships, round ships relied mainly on their sails. Oars were only for steering in harbour or when the wind dropped. The ships travelled long distances across the Mediterranean. The captain's greatest fear was being caught far out at sea when a storm was brewing.

GREEKS OVERSEAS

The Greeks traded with other peoples all around the Mediterranean Sea. In particular, there was a great deal of trade with Greek settlements overseas (colonies).

MAP KEY
■ Greek colonies

Round ships were designed to carry large loads, rather than for speed.

Most slaves were foreigners brought to Greece by professional dealers.

Slaves had no rights at all

HUMAN CARGO

Like other civilisations at that time, human slaves were bought and sold throughout the Greek world. Slaves had no choice but to work for the person who owned them. The unlucky ones ended up as mine workers. A trusted household slave, on the other hand, might live almost as one of the family.

WE MADE GOOD PROGRESS AT FIRST.

THEN THE WIND STRENGTHENED.

IS THIS DANGEROUS?

MAY THE GODS BLESS YOU – NO, SIR!

C-RR-AACK!

WE'VE SPRUNG A LEAK!

CRASSHH!

IT'S... NO... GOOD...

CAN'T STOP IT!

STORY CONTINUES ON NEXT PAGE

SHALL I **KILL** THEM NOW?

BUT **ONLY JUST.**

SMALL CHANGE

Each city-state made its own coins as a sign of its independence. Coins were usually highly decorative and were stamped with symbols of the Greek gods and goddesses. They were made of silver or, occasionally, gold.

Olive oil and wine were stored in long, narrow pottery jars called amphorae.

Decorated pottery

GOODS OUT

Olive oil and wine were the main products the Greeks sold abroad (exported). Most of their exports were things they had made. Greek wine, stored in large pottery jars, was always popular. Delightfully decorated Greek pottery was a valuable luxury. Greek metalwork, such as weapons and armour, was about the best available.

Unloading a cargo of timber

...AND GOODS IN

The Greek states needed goods brought in (imported) from their colonies. They were always short of timber, for instance. Extra corn was usually imported because local harvests were unreliable. Athens used its navy to control the grain trade.

ABANDON SHIP!

MAY **ATHENE** PRESERVE US!

I'VE GOT YOU FATHER...

IT SEEMED AN **IMPOSSIBLE** SWIM TO THE SHORE.

WE MADE IT...

25

CONTINUED FROM PREVIOUS PAGE

THESE ARE NO PIRATES, BOY.

WE HAD BEEN RESCUED BY HELOTS.

THEY HATED THEIR MASTERS, THE SPARTANS.

BUT SHOWED US MUCH KINDNESS.

NOW REST.

LIFE ON THE LAND

Farming was the most important job in all Greece. The way the land was farmed varied from place to place. In Sparta, for instance, citizens were allowed only to be soldiers, not farmers. Their land was looked after for them by workers called *helots*. These were labourers like those who rescued Kinesias and Pylades after the shipwreck.

Farming land in Greece was scarce because so much of the country was mountainous.

Women made bread every day.

The Ancient Greeks ate bread with every meal. To make bread, grain was pounded with heavy pestles in stone mortars, turning it into flour.

Sheep provided milk, meat and wool for making clothes.

SPARTA'S SLAVES

Helots were descendents of the people defeated by the Spartans in wars. They were farmers and were forced to give half of what they produced to their Spartan masters. The Spartans treated them very harshly.

SELF-SUFFICIENCY

Throughout Greece, farming households produced everything they needed. The family grew all their own food and made their own clothes. If they had any produce left over, they sold it in a nearby market.

Inner courtyard

WE LEFT OUR NEW-FOUND FRIENDS AT FIRST LIGHT.

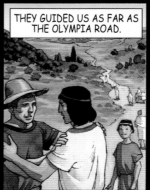

MAY THE GODS PROTECT YOU.

THEY GUIDED US AS FAR AS THE OLYMPIA ROAD.

WE JOINED THE OLYMPIC THRONG.

KINESIAS!

OUR FELLOW ATHENIANS WELCOMED US WARMLY.

CUNNING CATCH

Some Greek writers did not approve of fishing – they said it needed cunning, not 'manly' talents like skill or strength! Even so, fish was a key part of most Greeks' diet. The creatures were caught in nets or with a fishing rod and line. Large and sometimes dangerous species, like swordfish, were harpooned.

STORY CONTINUES ON NEXT PAGE

Cuttlefish were highly prized.

For most Greeks, eating fish was a rare treat.

GAME BIG AND SMALL

Lions once roamed the plains of Greece, but by Kinesias' time they had died out. Instead, hunters armed with bows, slings and spears went after wild boar. Deer and hares were less dangerous. Birds were hunted, too, often with nets or traps.

A hunter returns with his catch.

No country home was complete without a beehive. Honey had a thousand uses. For example, it could be added to beer, wine and bread, because it was the main source of sweetness.

HARD WORK

All country people grew their own vegetables such as cabbages, peas, onions and garlic. Greek poets painted a rosy picture of country life, but farming was actually extremely hard work.

Oxen were used to pull ploughs.

OR OULETES WILL TAKE CARE OF YOU!

YOU HAD BETTER BE...

DON'T WORRY, SIR. I - I'M TAKING CARE OF IT.

IT CAN'T BE...

TIME TO START TRAINING!

YOU'RE RIGHT!

WE HAVE A RACE TO WIN!

MEANWHILE, NOT FAR AWAY... WELCOME MYRTILOS. IS THE JOB DONE?

WELL...

KINESIAS! KINESIAS! KINESIAS!

OLYMPIC GAMES

The Olympic Games were the most famous athletic contests in ancient Greece. They were held every four years at Olympia and lasted for five days. The site was sacred to the god Zeus, who had been worshipped there for centuries before the games started. They were attended by 20,000 spectators from all over Greece. To win the games was an athlete's supreme ambition. Yet the prize was very simple – a leafy crown made of wild olive!

4 SPORTING EVENTS
All the contests, apart from horse races, took place at the *stadion* (track). Events included discus and javelin throwing, long jump, and wrestling.

3 BURNING ALTAR
At the great stone altar of Zeus, many oxen were sacrificed at the beginning of each games. Their thigh bones were burned on a vast pile of ashes in honour of Zeus. The athletes also sacrificed animals to the gods and swore that they would not cheat.

2 SACRED GROVE
The games took place in a sacred grove called the *altis*. Originally, the *altis* was a wooded field. Herakles was said to have cleared it and started games there in honour of his father, Zeus. For the first 50 years, the only event was a foot race to light the sacred fire that burned in Zeus' honour.

1 GYMNASIUM
Before the games began, the athletes trained in the gymnasium that stood beside the River Kladeios.

CONTINUED FROM PREVIOUS PAGE

WITH THE **FULL MOON**, THE GAMES FINALLY ARRIVED.

KINESIAS WAS IN PERFECT HEALTH AGAIN.

WE TOOK PART IN THE OPENING CEREMONY.

A HUNDRED OXEN WERE **SACRIFICED**...

FOR ZEUS' BLESSING.

WE WATCHED THE BOYS' GAMES.

THEN IT WAS NEARLY TIME FOR THE BIG RACE.

CAN I HELP YOU WITH YOUR **ARMOUR**, MASTER KINESIAS?

NO, JUST SOME WATER, PLEASE.

NOW'S MY CHANCE.

UMPH!

5 RUNNING TRACK

Running races were held at the *stadion*. The traditional race was a one *stadion* sprint. There were also races of two *stadia*, and long distance races of 20 or 24 lengths. An athlete who won all three – a three-timer – was a real hero!

6 RACE-IN-ARMOUR

One of the most exciting races was the race-in-armour. The 25 athletes who took part wore full armour, including helmets and heavy, round shields.

7 HORSE RACES

Horse and chariot races were held on a dusty track called the Hippodrome. Jockeys rode without saddles or stirrups. The basic horse race was over 1,200 metres (3,936 feet), while chariots travelled up to 12 km (7 miles). The prize for the winner of a chariot race was awarded to the owner of the horses, not to the charioteer.

8 SPECTATORS

Crowds of men came from all over Greece. Women were not allowed to attend the games, though they could enter their chariot teams. Unmarried women had games of their own.

9 TEMPLE OF ZEUS

The most impressive building on the site was the Temple of Zeus, which housed the large gold and ivory statue of Zeus. The sculpture was one of the 'seven wonders of the world'.

10 TOP HOTEL

This two-storey building was used to house important guests at the Olympic games.

11 SCULPTURE WORKSHOP

The famous sculptor Pheidias, who constructed the gigantic statue of Zeus, used a workshop on the site. The building beside the studio was the priests' house.

MYTHICAL HEROES

The ancient Greeks liked a good story. Best of all, they loved a thrilling yarn about heroes – men and women who were braver and more talented than ordinary folk. Such stories may have started out as true, but they were exaggerated each time they were told. Kinesias' victory over the Spartans, for example, was just the sort of story that might have been told many times, turning him into a hero.

1 THE NEMEAN LION
The first of Herakles' 12 labours was to kill this raging beast with weapon-proof skin. He strangled and skinned it with his bare hands!

2 THE LERNEAN HYDRA
This serpent monster had 12 heads. Whenever Herakles cut off one of them, two more grew in its place. In the end, he sealed the necks with fire.

3 THE HIND OF KERYNEIA
Herakles chased this sacred deer for a whole year. When it finally collapsed from exhaustion, he grabbed it and carried it home in triumph.

4 THE ERYMANTHIAN BOAR
This huge wild pig terrorized the people who lived near Mount Erymanthos. Our hero drove the animal into a snowdrift, jumped on its back and fastened it with chains.

5 THE STABLES OF KING AUGEIAS
This king's stables had not been cleaned for years. Faced with the task of cleaning up all the stinking muck in a day, Herakles washed the yard clean by diverting two rivers through it.

6 THE STYMPHALIAN BIRDS
Herakles sent these man-eating monsters mad with terror by clacking a pair of castanets given to him by the goddess Athene. Then he fired rocks at them with a sling.

7 THE FIRE-BREATHING BULL OF CRETE
Although offered help by King Minos, Herakles overcame the creature single-handed. Simple!

8 THE FLESH-EATING HORSES OF DIOMEDES
As King Diomedes was a bully, Herakles knocked him out and fed him to his own horses. No longer hungry, they allowed Herakles to ride them home.

9 QUEEN HIPPOLYTE'S BELT
Herakles killed the queen of the warrior women known as the Amazons and stole the famous belt that she wore in battle.

10 THE CATTLE OF GERYON
Geryon was a powerful monster who had three bodies. After shooting an arrow through all three of them, Herakles calmly walked off with his cattle.

11 THE APPLES OF THE HESPERIDES
To get hold of these valuable golden fruit, Herakles needed the help of Atlas, whose job was to support the world on his shoulders. Herakles held the world for a while while Atlas got the fruit.

12 KERBEROS IN THE UNDERWORLD
After a terrifying journey through the realm of ghosts and torment, Herakles throttled the three-headed dog Kerberos into submission and dragged him up to the surface.

HERAKLES THE HERO

Courageous strong-man Herakles (or Hercules) was the most famous mythical hero of ancient Greece. He was thought to be the son of the god Zeus by a human woman. Countless stories were told about him. The best known were his 12 Labours – near-impossible tasks demanded of him by the King of Argos after Herakles had killed his own children in a fit of rage.

THE RACE-IN-ARMOUR BEGAN.

HA! NOW FOR A TRAGIC ACCIDENT!

ARGHHHHH!

WHAT THE ....?!

NO!!

MAKE WAY!

SPARE HIS LIFE, O MERCIFUL GODS!

KINESIAS, HOW BADLY ARE YOU HURT...?

WHERE IS MY BROTHER?

WHAT!? YOU!!

MERCY! I'LL TELL ALL ...

LYKOURGOS PAID ME!

SEIZE HIM!

THESEUS AND THE MINOTAUR

Theseus was Athens' national hero. After several daring exploits, he volunteered to go to the kingdom of Minos on the island of Crete and kill the Minotaur. This monster was half-bull and half-man and it lived inside a labyrinth or maze. With the help of the beautiful Ariadne, Minos' daughter, Theseus entered the labyrinth, slew the Minotaur and found his way back to safety. On his return he was proclaimed king.

Medusa's severed head remained dangerous to anyone who looked at it.

WINGED AVENGER

Perseus was one of the bravest of Zeus' many children. His most daring deed was killing Medusa. The hair of this monstrous witch-like figure writhed with snakes and anyone she looked at would instantly be turned to stone. Perseus flew around the world on winged shoes in search of Medusa. He only ever looked at her reflection in his shiny shield – then he severed the lethal head.

Perseus' famous shield

Sickle (curved blade) used to cut off Medusa's head

HORSE PLAY

The *Iliad* and the *Odyssey*, famous poems by the Greek poet Homer, tell the story of the Greek war against the distant city of Troy. After battling unsuccessfully for 10 years, the Greeks finally tricked their way into the city. They built a huge wooden horse, left it outside the walls, and pretended to sail away. Curious about the horse, the Trojans dragged it into their city. Out jumped Greek soldiers! They opened the gates to let in their triumphant army.

The Trojans move the wooden horse into the city.

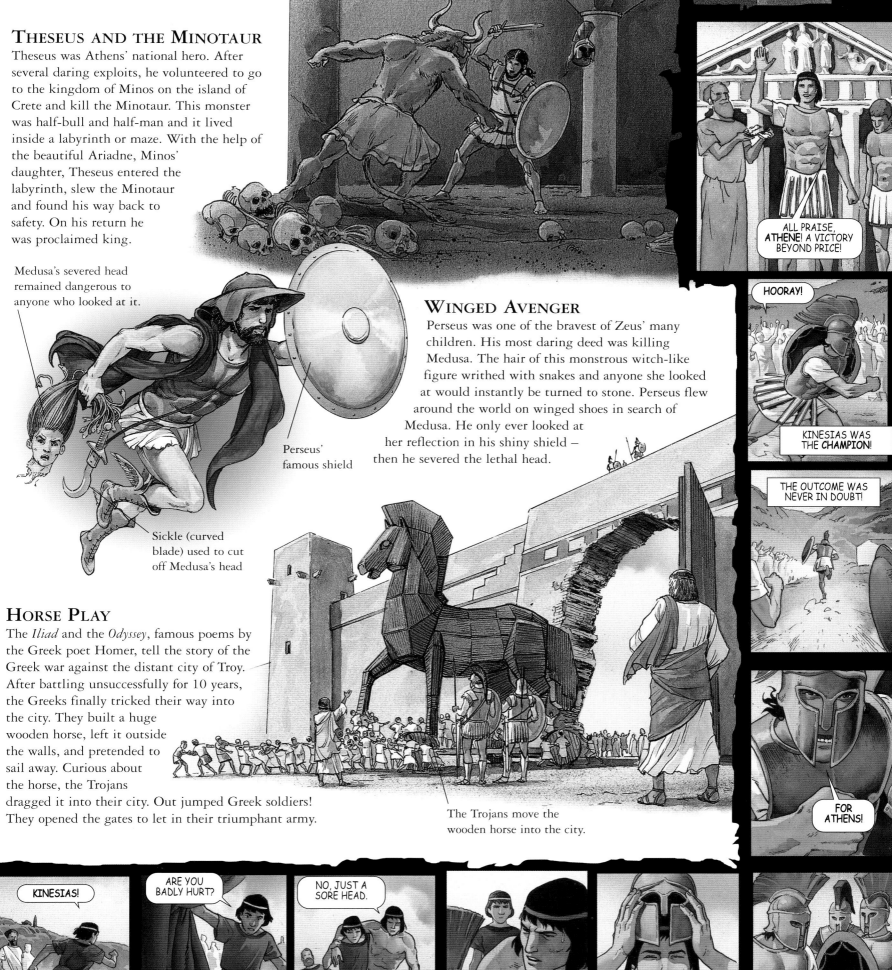

ALL PRAISE, ATHENE! A VICTORY BEYOND PRICE!

HOORAY!

KINESIAS WAS THE **CHAMPION**!

THE OUTCOME WAS NEVER IN DOUBT!

FOR ATHENS!

KINESIAS!

ARE YOU BADLY HURT?

NO, JUST A SORE HEAD.

THOUGH A LITTLE UNSTEADY...

HE WAS **DETERMINED** TO COMPETE.

THE RACE WAS RESTARTED.

INDEX